The Art of Sugarcraft

SUGARPASTE

The Art of Sugarcraft

SUGARPASTE

ANNE SMITH

Foreword Alison Procter
Series Editor Joyce Becker
Photography Graham Tann

MEREHURST PRESS
LONDON

Published 1987 by Merehurst Press
5 Great James Street
London WC1N 3DA

© Copyright 1987 Merehurst Limited

ISBN 0 948075 54 6

Designed by Carole Perks
Editorial Assistant Suzanne Ellis
Typeset by Filmset
Colour separation by Fotographics Ltd, London-Hong Kong
Printed by New Interlitho S.p.A., Milan

ACKNOWLEDGEMENTS
I could have not sustained the energy to persevere without the help of
my husband Clive, who has supported and encouraged me in many
ways, including acting as cook, nanny and chief bottle washer.
Also my grateful thanks to two very patient and understanding little
children, Helen and David.
Alison Procter initially planted the seeds of interest for this subject, first
when I saw her demonstrating her beautiful flowers, and later as my
tutor. I shall be eternally grateful for her generosity in sharing her
knowledge and ideas.

The Publishers would like to thank the following for their help and
advice:
Lucy Baker
Cuisena Cookware Limited
Elizabeth David Limited, 46 Bourne Street, London SW1W 8JD and
    at Covent Garden Kitchen Supplies, 3 North Row, The Market,
    Covent Garden, London WC2
Kim Golding
Guy Paul and Company Limited, Unit B4, A1 Industrial Park,
    Little End Road, Eton Scoton, Cambridgeshire, PE19 3JH
B.R. Mathews & Son, 12 Gipsy Hill, Upper Norwood, London
    SE19 1NN

Companion volumes:
The Art of Sugarcraft — **MARZIPAN**
The Art of Sugarcraft — **CHOCOLATE**
The Art of Sugarcraft — **PIPING**
The Art of Sugarcraft — **SUGAR FLOWERS**
The Art of Sugarcraft — **ROYAL ICING**
The Art of Sugarcraft — **PASTILLAGE AND SUGAR MOULDING**
The Art of Sugarcraft — **LACE AND FILIGREE**

CONTENTS

ANNE SMITH

Although an extremely gifted craftswoman, Anne Smith is fairly new to the art of sugarcraft. A qualified arts and crafts teacher with 15 years experience, she decided to study sugarcraft and cake decorating at an evening class so that she could make wonderful birthday cakes for her children. She brought her great skills as a sculptor, potter and needlewoman to this new medium, enjoyed it thoroughly, and was immediately successful. She joined the Avon branch of the British Sugarcraft Guild, and she won the sugarpaste class in the very first competition she entered, in 1985.

Anne has since gone on to learn more and more about sugarcraft, to perfect her techniques, and to win more prizes for her beautiful work. She particularly enjoys sugarpaste work because it uses her previous training and considerable skills in pottery, which she feels is closely related to sugarpaste modelling. She has now added cake decorating courses to her already full teaching commitments, and admits to enjoying these more than her other classes. She feels that sugarcraft is something which can be done well by everyone, at any age, and is a respected teacher whose attitude is 'never give up'. She hopes to take on more sugarcraft classes in the future, and plans to enter competitions at national and international level.

Welsh-born Anne Smith has lived for many years near Bath, England, where she has been Head of the Arts and Crafts Department at a Bristol comprehensive and has taught at Bath Technical College. She and her husband have a son and a daughter, who have fantastic, original cakes on every birthday.

FOREWORD

With so many books on the market about different aspects of cake decorating we could become quite bewildered, but here is a book on sugarpaste for the amateur or professional, a real delight and wonder for all.

Considering the relatively short time that Anne Smith has been working with sugarpaste, she has managed to bring so much enthusiasm to many original ideas, and a breath of life to old ones. Her artistic flair is much needed to give a new concept to an art form which could so easily become repetitive and unimaginative.

Anne is a delight to work with, and her training as an art teacher is apparent in her approach to the whole subject. I have never known anyone so prepared to go anywhere if there is a chance to learn something new. It is difficult for someone with young children to devote as much time as is needed, but somehow she manages it, and she is always appreciative of the support her family give her.

How nice to find a person who seems unaware of the extent of her natural talent.

This is a book that will give enjoyment as well as help with ideas and techniques. Anne's teaching ability makes her very sympathetic to the needs of the novice, as well as giving inspiration to the more experienced. I think the sugarcraft world is lucky to count Anne in its ranks as teacher, student and author, with her artistic flair from which so many will benefit.

ALISON PROCTER
Teacher, Demonstrator and National Judge

EQUIPMENT

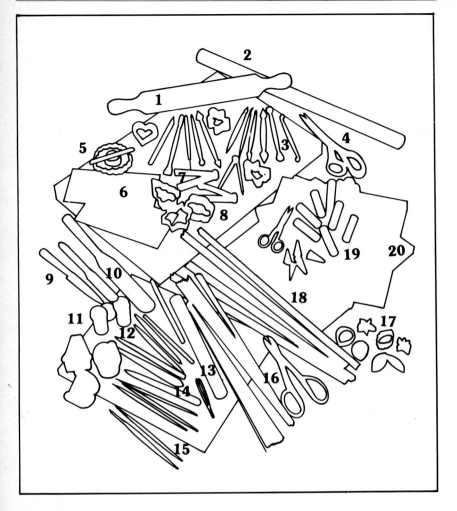

This is a selection of tools and equipment used for sugarpaste work. Most are ordinary kitchen or household items, while the more unusual tools are available from cake decorating shops and specialist shops.

1 Rolling pin and work surface
2 Greaseproof paper
3 Modelling tools
4 Scissors
5 Garrett frill cutter
6 Sugarpaste smoothers
7 Crimpers
8 Various pastry and cookie cutters
9 Kitchen knife
10 Palette knives
11 Paste colours
12 Sugarart pens
13 Small nonstick rolling pin and board
14 Anger tools
15 Paintbrushes
16 Floristry wire and wire cutters
17 Flower cutters
18 Piping tubes
19 Petal dust
20 Cake boards and cards

EQUIPMENT

The following basic tools and equipment can be used for sugarpaste work. Many are ordinary kitchen or household tools. The more specialist ones are:

☐ Worksurface. Melamine, nonstick plastic, marble or wood are suitable.

☐ Rolling pin. An extra long wooden or nonstick pin is necessary, plus a smaller stainless steel or nonstick pin for making plaques.

☐ Ball tools. A few different sizes are needed. A glass-headed pin can be used as a small ball tool.

☐ Knife. A good sharp cutting knife or scalpel is essential for trimming and cutouts.

☐ Scriber. Scraping and scratching fine lines is done with a scriber.

☐ Scissors. A pair of good fine-bladed scissors is necessary.

☐ Palette knives. Crank-handled and straight palette knives are used for lifting, trimming and smoothing.

☐ Wooden dowelling, smooth knitting needles without heads, paintbrush handles. These are invaluable for pulled flowers and modelling.

☐ Spacers. These ensure the correct overall thickness of paste or marzipan when rolling out.

☐ Cutters. Use flower, pastry and biscuit cutters for making plaques and cutouts. Frills and flounces are made with Garrett frill cutters.

☐ Crimpers and leather embossing tools. Use these for decorating soft sugarpaste.

☐ Modelling tools. Buy these or adapt and make tools to create the various effects you want.

☐ Colours. Dry dusting colours, paste colours and liquid food colours are necessary.

☐ Cake boards and polystyrene dummies. The latter are useful for practice.

☐ Florist's wire. You will need varying gauges for flower work and forming armaments for models.

☐ Paper and card. Greaseproof and silicone paper are used for icing bags and runouts; thin card is used for templates.

☐ Piping tubes. Various sizes and shapes are available in nickel plate or plastic. The former are more expensive but the sizing tends to be more accurate.

☐ Brushes. Use sable hair brushes. Keep separate the brushes needed for fine paintwork, brush embroidery and cocoa painting.

☐ Tweezers. Use fine pointed ones with grooved ends.

☐ Smoothers. These are used for smoothing marzipanned and sugarpasted cakes.

RECIPES

Recipe for sugarpaste

> 900g (2lb/8 cups) icing
> (confectioner's) sugar
> 125ml (4fl oz/½ cup) glucose
> 15g (½oz) gelatine
> 25g (¾oz) glycerine
> 50ml (2fl oz/¼ cup) cold water

Soak the gelatine in the cold water and place over hot water until dissolved and clear. (Do not allow the gelatine to boil.)

Add the glycerine and glucose to the gelatine. Stir until melted. Add mixture to sieved sugar. Knead to a soft consistency.

Recipe for modelling paste

This paste is malleable and easily stretched which makes it ideal for bas relief.

> 250g (9oz/2¼ cups) icing
> (confectioner's) sugar
> 15ml (1 level tablespoon) gum
> tragacanth
> 5ml (1 tsp) liquid glucose
> 30ml (6 tsp) cold water

Sieve the sugar with the gum tragacanth. Add the liquid glucose and cold water to the sugar and mix well. Knead to form a soft dough.

Combine with an equal weight of sugarpaste. Leave 24 hours before using.

If the paste is dry, work in a little white fat (shortening) or egg white as needed. If the paste is sticky, add cornflour (cornstarch) as needed.

BASIC TECHNIQUES

Most beginners can successfully cover a cake with sugarpaste but a professional finish — a glossy surface free of cracks and air bubbles with smooth rounded corners — will only result from practice. Try not to cover a cake under artificial light as flaws are not as clearly defined as in daylight. It is difficult to hide any imperfections on the covering as these may occur where you don't want to add decorations. Don't panic if the covering starts to go wrong; it can always be removed and reapplied.

Although sugarpaste can be homemade, many cake decorators now use commercial sugarpaste, which is of a particularly good firm quality.

There are many techniques that can be used to decorate the covered cake. Crimping, embos-sing and ribbon insertion are done when the paste is still soft. These simple techniques may help hide the imperfections of a poor surface.

More advanced techniques are bas relief and appliqué, the addition of frills and flounces, emboidery and lace.

Store unused paste in a plastic bag or airtight container in a cool, dry place.

The sugarpaste on the cake will soon skin, or become firm on the surface. Store the cake in a dry place out of direct sunlight which may fade the colours. A cardboard box is the ideal container; a sealed plastic container causes the cake to sweat and the icing may not skin.

Colouring sugarpaste
Adding colour to sugarpaste is better done in natural light, as artificial light can affect colour perception.

Add a little at a time; more can always be added later. If the colour is too dark, add another piece of paste and knead again. A pale base colour generally looks more pleasing and nicely sets off the colours of the flowers, ribbons, and other decorations.

To colour a large amount of paste, divide into small pieces, colour each one, then knead all the pieces together to blend.

After kneading in the colour, cut the paste in half to see if streaks are visible. If so, re-knead and cut again until all streaking has disappeared.

Streaks can however be used to create a marbled effect. To achieve this, colour is kneaded into the paste slightly. When the paste is rolled out, the surface has a definite streaky pattern.

COVERING THE CAKE

A sugarpasted cake must have smooth rounded edges and corners. To achieve this, the covering is applied in one piece.

Gently heat some apricot jam purée and brush over the surface of the cake to ensure that the covering will stick.

Applying marzipan
Knead the marzipan until pliable.

Knead on a clean dry work surface with a circular motion so that the edge of the paste is brought into the middle, forming pleats. The lower surface remains quite smooth. When rolling out, this smooth side should be uppermost.

Roll out on a surface evenly dusted with icing (confectioner's) sugar. Never use flour or cornflour (cornstarch) as these can cause fermentation.

Keep the marzipan moving so it does not stick but don't turn it over. Roll out to the shape of the cake. The use of marzipan spacers at this stage ensures that the overall thickness of the marzipan is constant.

Measure the cake with a piece of string; up one side, across the top and down the other side. The marzipan should be rolled out a little larger than this measurement.

Carefully remove greaseproof paper, taking care not to damage the corners. Turn cake upsidedown to provide a good flat surface and stick on a board with a little softened marzipan. If the edges of the cake do not sit level on the cake board, make a sausage of marzipan and push into the gaps with a palette knife. Fill any visible holes and repair damaged corners with marzipan. Smooth over the cake.

To apply, lift up the left side of the marzipan and lay it over your right arm. Lift your arm and drape the bottom of the marzipan against the side of the cake; the right side of the marzipan should still be on the board. Drape over the top of the cake, transfer marzipan to the left hand and support it while you remove air bubbles by brushing your right hand across the top of the cake.

Skirt out the corners and, using the flat of your hand, smooth the marzipan to the sides of the cake with an upward movement. If a downward movement is used, it drags the marzipan and weakens the paste at the corners and edges. Use smoothers to eliminate any finger marks and bumps. Smooth the corners and upper edge using your warm hands. Place the flat edge of a cranked palette knife against the cake at the base and cut away excess

Applying the sugarpaste

The cake does not need to be covered with marzipan first. It can, if preferred, be covered in two layers of sugarpaste instead. The first layer is usually thinner and should be allowed to skin and harden before adding the final layer. Both layers are applied in the same way.

Knead the sugarpaste as for marzipan, kneading in colour if using.

Roll out the sugarpaste on a light dusting of icing (confectioner's) sugar. Too much sugar will dry the paste and make it crack. Use the spacers to keep the thickness of the paste uniform. Measure the cake as for marzipan and roll out the sugarpaste a little larger all round.

Before applying the paste, sterilize the surface of the cake by wiping the marzipan with clear spirit such as gin, vodka or kirsch. Using the palm of your hand or a brush, make sure the entire surface is moist. If there are any dry patches, the paste may not stick to the marzipan and an air bubble could result.

Drape sugarpaste over cake.

Lift and drape the paste over the cake using the same technique as for marzipan. Skirt out the corners and smooth out any creases using an upward movement. Remember that rings or long fingernails could mark the surface. Use smoothers to rub over the top and sides of the cake and to round the corners.

If any air bubbles have been trapped under the paste, insert a clean needle into the bubble at an angle. Smooth over with your hand to expel the air and rub with a smoother. If the pin hole is still visible, this can be easily hidden with a small dot of icing of the same colour piped into the hole and then wiped away to leave a smooth finish.

Smooth and cut at base.

Using a cranked palette knife, trim excess paste away carefully and smooth over cut area.

Using your hand, rub the top of the cake until it feels like silk and round edge in the same way.

Wipe away any sugar on the board and store the cake in a dry place until the sugarpaste has skinned and you are ready to decorate it. The ideal container is a cardboard box.

A cake with marbled sugarpaste.

HEART CAKE

A heart-shaped cake, suitable for
a small wedding, decorated with
crimper work and topped with a
sugar orchid. Fresh or silk flowers
could also be used.

EMBOSSING

Embossing is similar to crimper work, as it also must be done while the sugarpaste is fresh. The two techniques can be used in conjunction with each other.

Many different tools can be used to impress a pattern into the paste. Leather embossing tools, which are available in many different patterns, are very effective. These can be purchased from craft shops. Decorative spoon handles can produce interesting effects. To add delicate finishing touches to small scallops and flowers, try using the tops of icing tubes.

Embossing can be used on the cake board as well as the cake. It also looks effective as an edging around a plaque.

Both crimper work and embossing can be used effectively with other techniques such as embroidery and ribbon insertion. Colour can be added by picking out areas with edible dusting powder or painting with food colour.

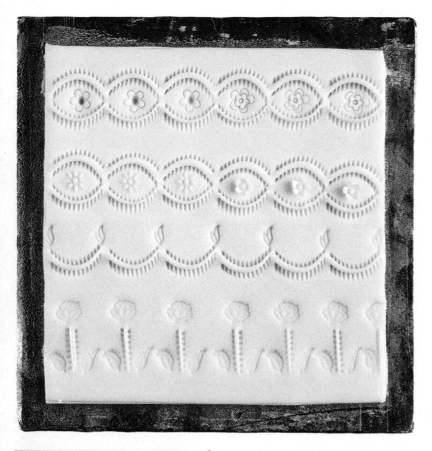

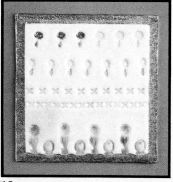

Crimper work and embossing used together.

CRIMPING

Crimpers are stainless steel tools used to impress and pinch a design onto soft freshly applied sugarpaste. It is a technique that beginners can easily master to produce a professional finish, and it is an ideal way of disguising marks on a poorly finished cake. Practise beforehand on a spare piece of sugarpaste.

Crimping can be done on any part of the cake but is most effective used on the top edge or the sides. Use crimper work sparingly, or the cake will look cluttered.

Crimpers are available in nine different designs: oval, curve, scallop, double scallop, diamond, vee, straight line, heart and holly.

To ensure adequate control of the crimpers, twist an elastic band around the head of the tool, positioned a quarter of the way down the arms. This makes sure the crimpers do not spring open when in use and tear the paste.

Mark the position of the pattern on the cake by using a paper template at   to the sides of the cake, or   out the design using pin pricks.

Dip the serrated end of the crimper into cornflour (cornstarch) occasionally so that it does not stick to the paste. Insert crimpers into the sugarpaste and pinch together, release slowly and withdraw the crimpers. It is important to release the crimpers slowly and remove carefully each time, as the paste can easily be torn or pulled too far from the cake, making the pattern irregular. Crimp the pattern around the cake.

Crimping can be used as a border around the base of a cake, especially by beginners who might lack confidence to pipe a border with royal icing. Simply roll out a thin sausage of paste, long enough to go around the cake. Cut the sausage ends at an angle, place round the cake and butt the ends together. Then crimp the border.

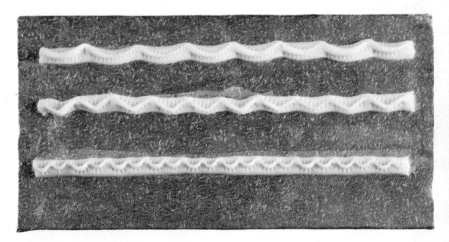

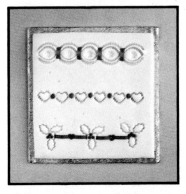

Above: crimper work borders.
Below: crimper designs for cake sides.

Above: embossing with piping tubes combined with crimper designs.

Below: Crimper work designs for Christmas cakes.

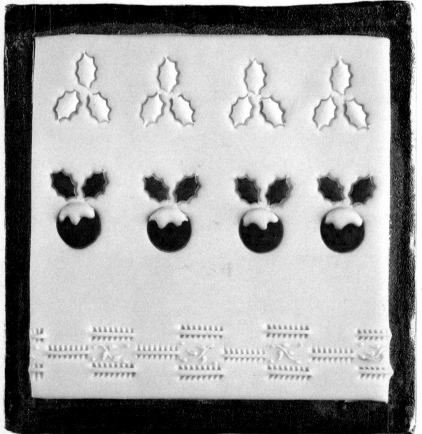

RIBBON INSERTION

This technique creates the illusion that ribbon has been threaded through the sugarpaste. The width of the ribbon can range from very fine to about 1cm (⅜in). For an elegant effect choose colours to match the sugarpaste and embroidery. Contrasting colours will result in a brighter look.

The section where the ribbon is to be placed should be measured first and marked with either a pin or scriber so that the lines are straight and the ribbon lengths will be separated by equal spaces of icing.

Insert the ribbon while the sugarpaste is still soft. Make a slit in the paste using a scalpel or ribbon inserting tool. Take care

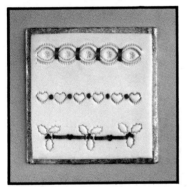

that the slit is not so deep that it reaches the marzipan beneath the sugarpaste. (See below)

For narrow ribbon inserts, fold a piece of ribbon about 1cm (⅜in) long in half and place in the slit with tweezers.

For wider ribbon inserts cut the ribbon slightly longer than the space between the slits. The ribbon should be long enough so that it makes a loop and does not lie flat on the cake. Each loop should be the same distance away from the cake. Experiment with the first piece of ribbon and when satisfied, carefully remove it so as not to damage the slits and cut all the pieces to this length.

Moisten each cut edge of ribbon with a little egg white and then use tweezers to place one edge in each slit.

Ribbon insertion looks effective with other techiques such as crimping, broderie anglaise and lacework. Lace pieces can be applied between the loops of ribbon or attached to the edge or edges of flat ribbon banding. Embroidery can be piped onto the ribbon, or onto the cake to give the appearance of holding the ribbon in place.

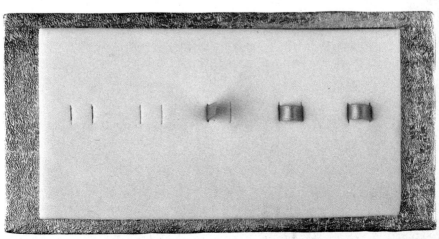

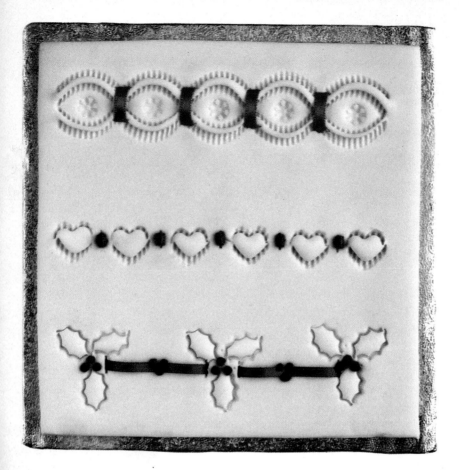

Crimper work, ribbon insertion
and piped embroidery.

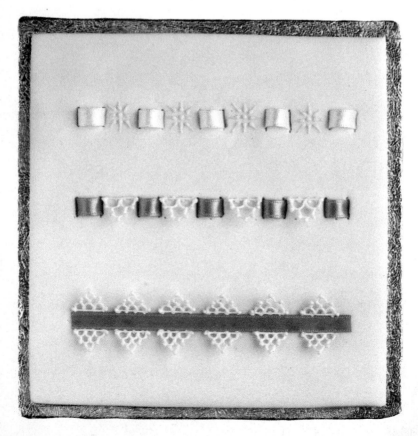

RIBBON BANDING

Banding is a way of using ribbon to finish off a cake and bring out one or two of its colours. Ribbons in different shades of the same colour make a lovely subtle effect.

The bands of ribbon should be applied when the sugarpaste is dry. Pipe dots of icing onto the cake and place the ribbon on top immediately. Hide the join where the two ends overlap with a small neat bow in the same colour.

Stagger the bows so that they are not one above the other as this would make the cake look cluttered.

WEDDING BELLS

The frilled and embroidered bells
could be displayed as shown, or
placed on a perspex cake stand.

BRODERIE ANGLAISE

Broderie anglaise is a delicate technique so take care at the piping stage. Various tools may be used to indent the soft sugarpaste. Use the pointed end of a knitting needle or the rounded end of a paintbrush to obtain the correct size hole. The leaf or petal shape can be made by pinching a writing tube (No8 or smaller) into the correct shape with a pair of pliers. Fill the end of the tube with modelling paste and let dry.

Make the pattern holes in the sugarpaste and leave to skin. Pipe round the edges of the indentations with a fine tube. The broderie anglaise can be coloured either by painting inside the indented shapes or using a little edible dusting powder. Take care to apply the colour so that it does not mark the surface of the cake. Another method would be to use coloured icing for piping. Whatever the method, keep to pastel shades.

Ideas for patterns can be found by looking at broderie anglaise fabric or trim. To give the raised satin stitch effect seen on some cloth, use soft peak royal icing. Pipe quite a lot on the edge of the flower and brush towards the centre with a fine damp sable brush so that it has that heavy rounded satiny appearance.

The plaques on these pages show different styles of broderie anglaise.

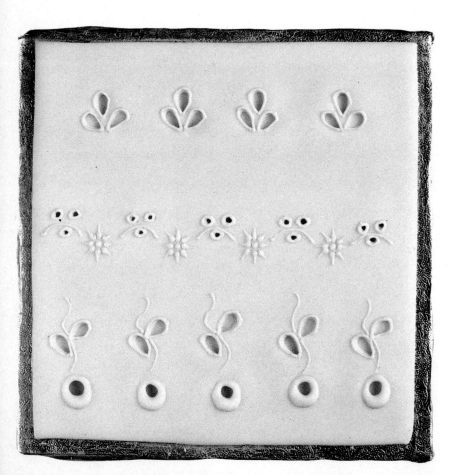

CHRISTENING CAKE

This Christening cake features layers of delicate frills. The bas relief baby is covered with a hand-painted quilt.

GARRETT FRILL

Frills and flounces are a delicate finishing touch on a cake. The frill is the invention of Elaine Garrett, a South African cake decorator.

Special round or straight cutters with scalloped edges are used to create the frill.

Knead 5ml (1tsp) gum tragacanth into 450g (1lb) sugarpaste and leave for at least 24 hours. This will enable the frill to keep its lift without drooping when placed on the cake.

Frills are easier to place on a firm surface, so allow the sugarpaste on the cake to dry for a few days.

If a crimped edge is desired, the frill must be applied when the paste on the cake is soft. This crimping can disguise a poor edge.

Before applying the frill pipe a snailstrail around the base of the cake. It is important that this edge is finished off neatly as it will be visible at the points where the frill lifts.

Roll the paste thinly and cut out a circle with a scalloped cutter. Remove a centre circle of paste. The size of this removed circle determines the width of the frill. Cut out a large inside circle for a narrow frill and a small inside circle for a deeper one.

Cut the frill and open up the circle until fairly straight. Be careful with the middle area of the upper edge as this is the weakest point.

Scribe a line onto the cake where the frill is to be attached. Place the frill near the edge of the board. Put a cocktail stick halfway up the paste and, putting an index finger on top of the stick, rotate it. As the stick moves forward over the paste it will make the frill. Repeat along the entire edge of the paste.

Moisten the cake below the scribed line with a litttle water and attach the frill. Smooth over the upper edge gently with your thumb. Raise the frill with the end of a paintbrush to give lift where needed. When adding the second frill, butt the edges together and turn under the extreme edge of the frill so that it appears to form a natural fold.

Several methods can be used to finish off the upper edge of the frill. Try piping a snailstrail, crossstitch or dots. Small lace sections can look very attractive. Plunger cutter flowers also produce a pleasing effect.

For a more definite lift use a flouncing or anger tool rotated gently in the same manner on the edge of the paste.

The cake's colour scheme can be emphasised by graduating the shade of each layer of frills, starting with the darkest shade for the lowest layer. Petal dusting powder can also be applied to the edge of the frill.

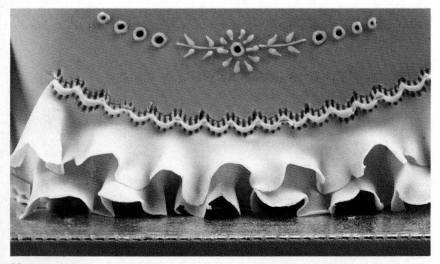

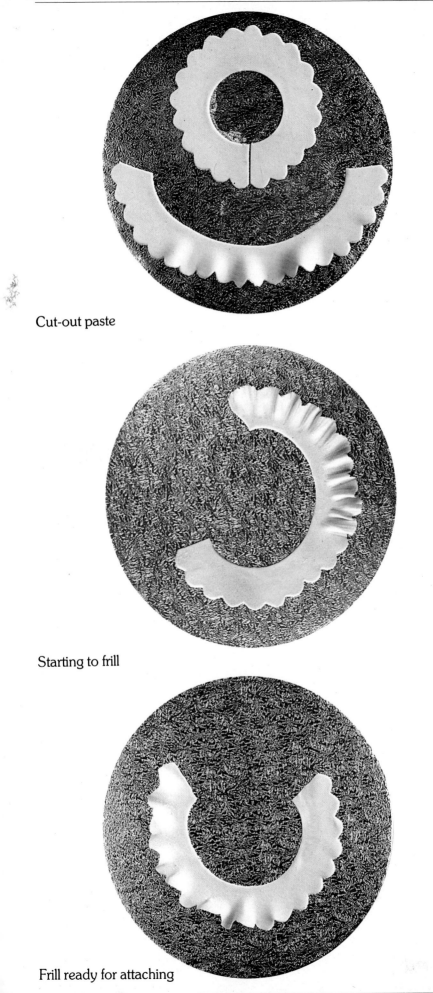

Cut-out paste

Starting to frill

Frill ready for attaching

Scribe a line on the cake

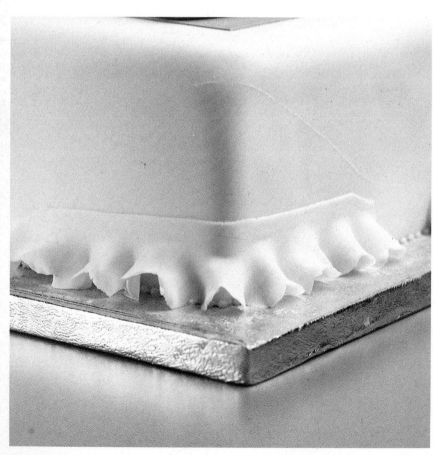

Single frill

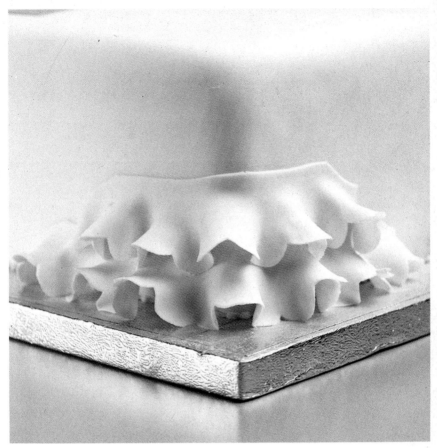

Double frill

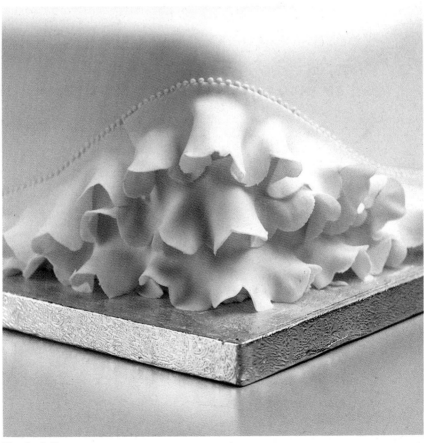

Triple frill

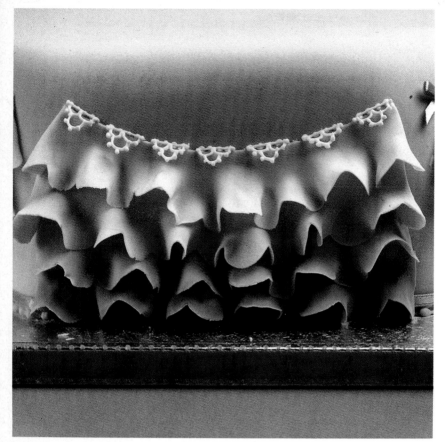

Tiered coloured frills

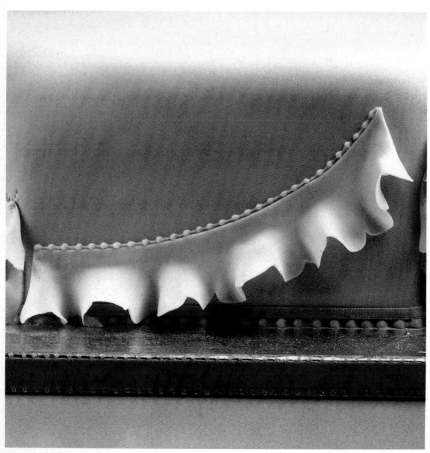

Curved single frill

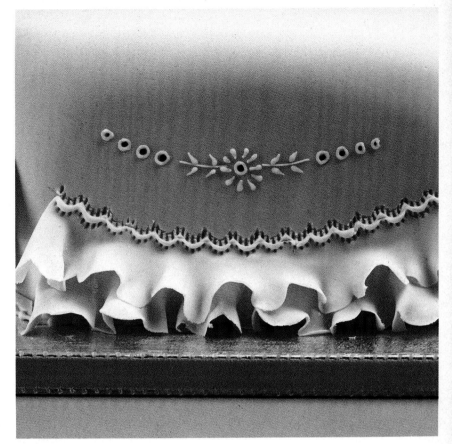

Frills and broderie anglaise

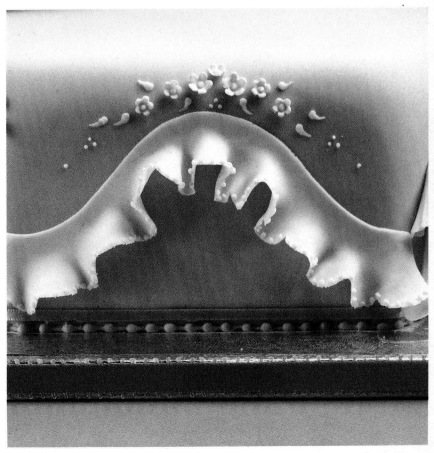

Scalloped frill

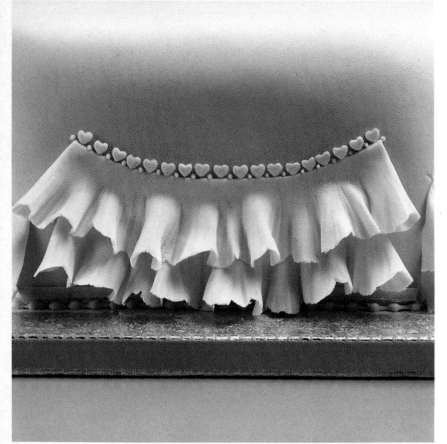

Double frill with appliquéd heart motif.

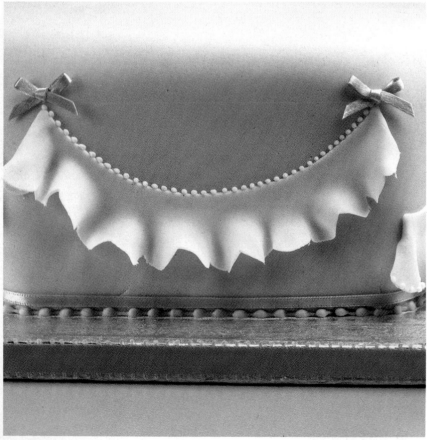

Single frill with bows

THE DRAPE

A drape can be used in conjunction with the Garrett frill or on its own on a plain cake. Knead 5ml (1 tsp) gum tragacanth into 450g (1lb) sugarpaste and leave for at least 24 hours.

Make a paper template larger than the cake board. The drape on the cake illustrated is 33cm (13in) in diameter; the cake board is 27.5cm (11in). Measure out six points on the edge of the template. Mark the six points on the cake. Roll out the sugarpaste on cornflour (cornstarch) until it is almost transparent.

Place the template on the paste and cut around it with a tracing wheel to make an attractive edge.

To attach the drape it is not necessary to moisten either cake or paste. Match up the six marks. Lift the side of the drape and secure with a cocktail stick at each of the six marks. When dry remove the sticks by twisting before pulling out.

CAKE WITH A DRAPE

An unusual birthday cake features a drape decorated with fine embroidery. Position sprays of sugar flowers at the points of the drape.

CUTWORK

Cutwork is a technique in which biscuit, aspic and flower cutters are used to create simple sugarpaste shapes. More original and intricate designs can be achieved if cardboard templates are used.

If using templates make them out of fine card, such as the sides of cereal boxes, as this is durable and has a firm edge against which to place the scalpel when cutting. This will give a clean, sharp edge to the paste which is most important in cutwork. Use a sharp craft knife or scalpel. Nothing will spoil the overall effect more than indistinct shapes or damaged lines.

Template for lettering

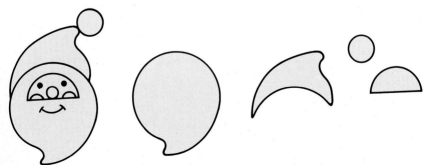

Templates for Father Christmas pieces

Cutwork designs for Christmas cakes.

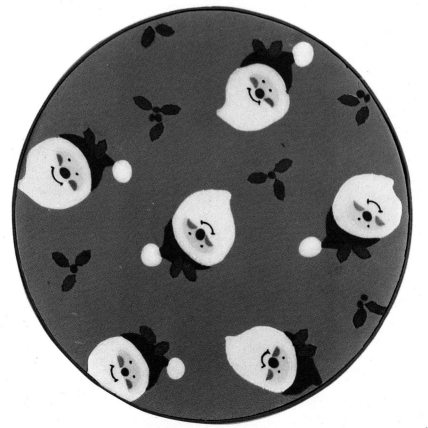

CLOWN

Make cardboard templates for all pattern shapes. Start painting the background and work forward. Keep the colours fresh and bright. Add finishing touches by painting in clothes, shoes, etc. Remember that the brush colours will not be true when applied to coloured paste. For example yellow paint will become green if put on blue paste. Therefore if a lot of the pattern is to be painted on, it is better to cut out the shapes in white paste.

Finished plaque

Template

CHRISTMAS TREE

Cut out the Christmas tree and
pot. Make small templates and
cut out enough shapes to fully
decorate tree.

Finished plaque

Template

PARCEL CAKE

The Christmas parcel is wrapped
with a sheet of cutwork sugarpaste
and tied with a big red ribbon
bow.

SUGARPASTE CONFECTIONERY

The possibilities for creating imaginative confectionery are endless.

Colour the sugarpaste and add flavour by using essences or oils to match the colours. For example, add orange oil to orange coloured sugarpaste, lemon oil to yellow paste, peppermint oil to green and coffee essence to brown.

When rolling out the sugarpaste use marzipan spacers to ensure the sweets will be a uniform thickness. Stamp out shapes using cookie cutters.

To decorate, some shapes can be half dipped in melted chocolate or piped with chocolate or royal icing. Make a small hole in some shapes and when dry thread with ribbon to hang on a Christmas tree. Small bars can be decorated as dominoes or traffic signals.

Completely immerse some sugarpaste circles in chocolate. When set small moulded animals, half dipped in chocolate, can be placed on top.

Traffic lights

Christmas tree ornaments

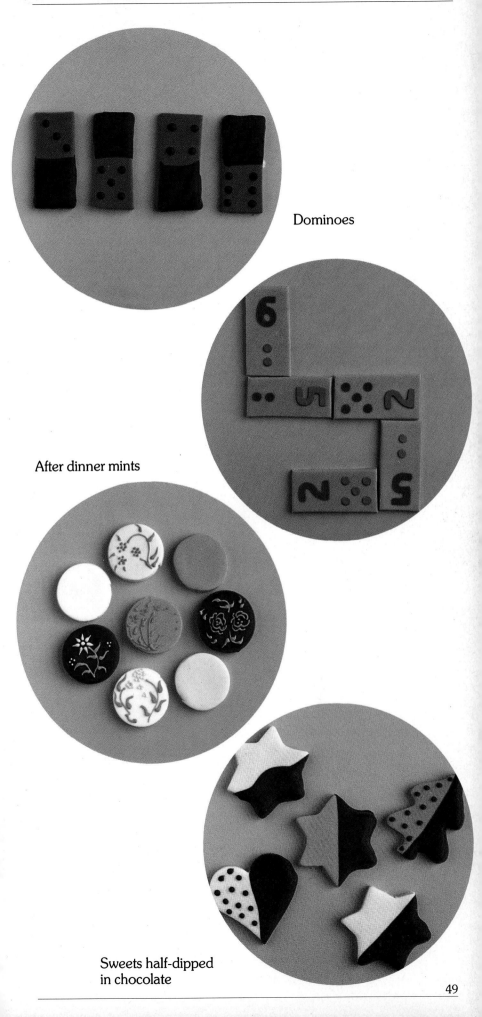

Dominoes

After dinner mints

Sweets half-dipped
in chocolate

49

Pencil
Roll a long sausage of pale wood coloured paste. Taper one end to form point. Roll out a thin piece of coloured paste. Wrap around wood piece and roll again to obliterate join. Roll a very small piece of coloured paste around the point of the pencil to form the lead.

Pen
Roll a long sausage of coloured paste for pen. Cut out a small piece of paste and wrap around the upper end of the pen to form cap. Roll carefully to obliterate join but do not flatten the thicker cap end. Roll a very fine sausage for the clip and attach with glue. When dry, paint clip with non-toxic gold.

Pig
Make a fat pink cone. Shape one end for the snout and mark the face. Attach ears and curly tail. Dip in melted chocolate and place on a round base.

Hedgehog
Make a fat brown cone and mark the face. Dip in melted chocolate, then add slivered almond 'spines'. Place on a round base.

Frog
Make a fat green cone, cut for the mouth and add a pink tongue. Make fat sausages for legs, shape and attach with melted chocolate. Place on a round base. Pipe eyes.

PARTY FACES

Party faces can be added to take-home bags at children's parties or used as place markers with each child's name tied round the neck.

Fill small petite four cases with melted chocolate to act as a heavy base and a neck. Colour some sugarpaste with flesh colour. Make a ball, indent eye sockets and add a tiny ball of paste for the nose. Leave to dry.

Paint on features, trying to vary the expressions. Add frills, hats, etc. Make hair by piping with chocolate or by pushing paste through a clean garlic press.

Each clown can have a different face.

FOX CUB CAKE

The cocoa-painting fox cub
plaque can be removed and saved
as a souvenir of the occasion.

COCOA PAINTING

Cocoa painting, a method similar to painting in oils, is an easy way to decorate a cake. The design can be painted directly onto the surface of the cake, or onto a sugarpaste, gelatine or marzipan plaque. The latter method enables the painting to be kept as a souvenir of the occasion, as the plaque can be removed before the cake is cut.

It is best to tint the plaque a shade of cream, as this colour blends nicely with brown. Beginners could start by copying a card or picture whose design is printed in sepia (brown) tones.

The design should not be drawn in detail, just the features and a rough outline. Too many lines will spoil the finished result as they tend to show through the cocoa where the tones are light.

Cocoa butter can be used but

this is difficult to find and expensive. Coconut oil produces the same effect and is easily available from health food shops.

If you don't wish to paint freehand, you can easily trace a picture onto the plaque. First trace the design onto the tracing paper. Turn the tracing paper over and retrace the image on the back using a brown lip pencil.

Place the paper on the plaque, right sides uppermost. Using a scribe or similar pointed tool, retrace the lines. The design should then be visible on the plaque.

Put a teaspoon of coconut oil into each of four containers. Place the containers into a shallow pan of hot water, then add a little cocoa to the first container, a little more to the second and even more to the third. You should have three distinct tones. In the fourth pot make a dark concentrated mixture to define eyes and shadows. While painting, re-heat the water if the mixtures become too stiff. If you must leave the design before its completion simply cover the pots and store. To use again, place the pots in hot water and stir well, as the cocoa colour tends to separate.

Start by covering the image and surrounding background in the palest tone.

Next paint in the medium tone.

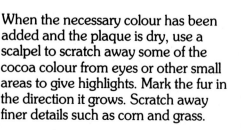

Proceed to more clearly defined areas using the darkest of the three tones. Leave the plaque to dry. Apply the final very dark concentrated colour to the pupils of the eyes, whiskers, deepest shadows, etc.

When the necessary colour has been added and the plaque is dry, use a scalpel to scratch away some of the cocoa colour from eyes or other small areas to give highlights. Mark the fur in the direction it grows. Scratch away finer details such as corn and grass.

Country village scene

Persian cat

Baby owl

Puppies

CAT CAKE

Paint the cat directly on the
surface of the cake, then frame
the painting with moulded flowers
and grass.

PAINTING ON SUGARPASTE

Beginners often use conventional colour schemes. By experimentation and trial and error a good sense of colour should develop and more creative designs should be possible.

Avoid the temptation to use colour straight from the container as few of these basic colours are true to nature. Experiment with colour by mixing.

Harmonious colours are used to give a balanced appearance to a cake. Colours from opposite sides of the colour wheel can be used together to create a striking effect, as long as one of the colours is used for detail only.

It is possible to paint directly onto the surface of completely dry sugarpaste. Use paste or liquid food colour. If painting for the first time do not paint directly onto the cake's surface as it is difficult to remove mistakes. Instead paint onto a plaque which can be placed on a cake if wished.

When applying colour to sugarpaste, keep the brush fairly dry. Too much moisture will cause streaking and may affect the surface of the paste.

If painting a scene, subtle blending of colour can be achieved by brushing one colour into the next while both are still wet.

If a pattern or quilt with clear defined lines is to be painted, one colour should be completely dry before an adjacent colour or surface pattern is applied.

If you plan to duplicate a favourite cake, make a note of how a certain colour has been achieved. This applies to painting onto paste as well as mixing colour into paste.

PLAQUES

Plaques are convenient when decorating a cake in a hurry as they can be prepared in advance. As long as they are stored correctly, preferably in a cardboard box in a dry place, they will last indefinitely. A plaque mounted on a velvet covered cake board or a wooden base would be a unique gift. Choose a design that can be used for a number of different occasions. A message suitable for the event can be piped on when the plaque is to be used.

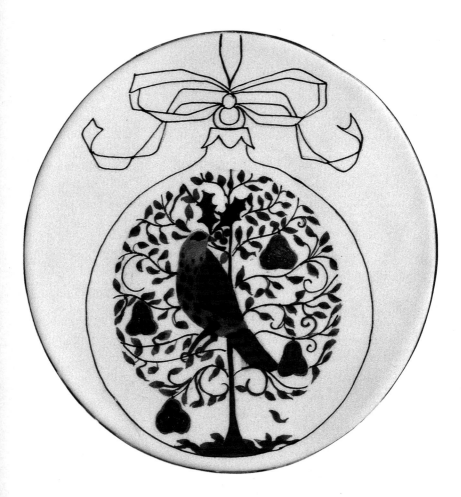

Partridge in a pear tree

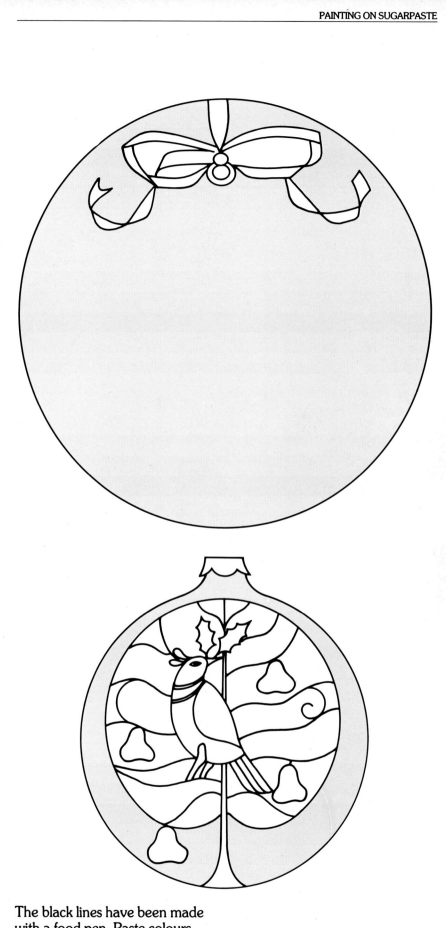

The black lines have been made with a food pen. Paste colours have been used for the tree and bird and non-toxic gold for the pears.

LETTERING

When attempting lettering it is important to take time to work out details such as layout, spacing and position on the cake or plaque. Always use good quality brushes ranging in size from No0 to No0000.

Practice, patience and a steady hand make perfect lettering.

Lettering looks wonderful highlighted with non-toxic gold or silver paint. Small flowers can also add to the overall effect.

Template for Congratulations

Plaques with lettering

CLOCK CAKE

This children's party cake tells the
tale of Hickory Dickery Dock. The
clock shape is created with a
sugarpaste collar.

COLLARS

Although collars are traditionally made of royal icing, which is strong and firm, they can also be made of sugarpaste. If you plan to make a complete collar without cutout areas sugarpaste would be strong enough without using any additives. However, any collar that has sections removed needs added strength. This can be done by adding gum tragacanth powder in the proportion 5ml (1tsp) to 450g (1lb) sugarpaste. Knead in well and rest for 24 hours before use.

Finished collars should be left for approximately a week to dry before placing on the cake. Turn

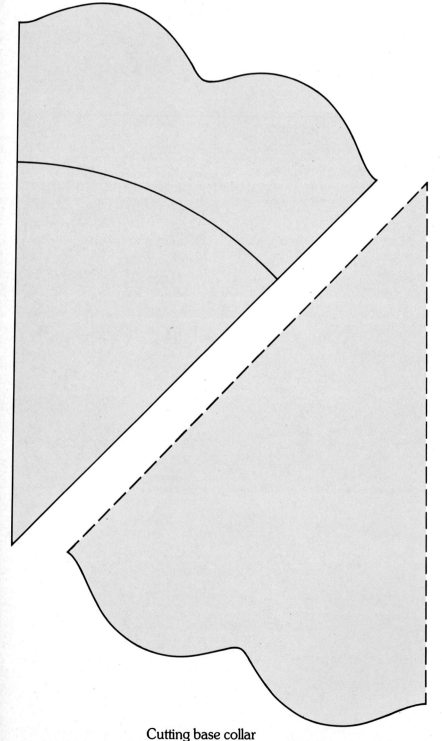

Cutting base collar

occasionally to allow the under-side to dry.

If the cake is fairly detailed the collar is better left undecorated as a contrast. However, a sugarpaste collar can be decorated by indenting a pattern or crimping the edges, decorating with broderie anglaise or appliqué.

Half template for top collar

CLOCK CAKE WITH COLLAR

The template for the larger of the two collars was made by cutting a paper octagon the same size as the cake board.

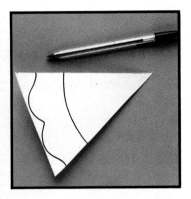

Divide the shape into eight sections by drawing lines from the points to the centre. Fold along the lines and cut the outer edge into two scallops, so that the folded shape resembles a heart.

Roll out the sugarpaste and cut around the template. Mark in the eight lines dividing the sections with the back of a long knife and leave to dry on a flat surface.

The template for the second collar is an octagon. Roll out the paste and cut around the template using a sharp kitchen knife. Leave to dry.
Make a small collar using a template cut from a part of one section of the first template. Leave to dry. To assemble attach the largest collar to the cake board with royal icing. Sugarpaste the cake and when the surface has dried place on top of the collar.

Cover a small piece of cake with sugarpaste and attach to the side of the cake. Remove a small circle of icing from above this with a small biscuit cutter so that the mouse and pendulum appear to be inside the cake.

Scribe the numerals onto the face of the clock. Paint in the background using paste or food colour, then outline and flood in the numbers. Make clock hands and lock in runout royal icing. Attach top collar.

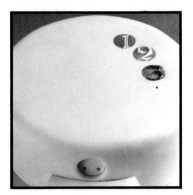

Make pendulum and hinge and attach. Paint numbers, hinge, lock and pendulum gold. Make feet and tail of mouse (see page 100) and place on pendulum.

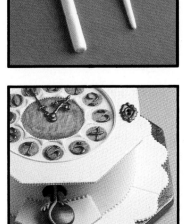

Decorate the edges of both collars with piping.

COURTING COUPLE CAKE

Bas relief is used to make the
courting couple three-dimensional
The pink frill has been hand-
painted to match the girl's dress.

BAS RELIEF

Bas relief is a technique which will produce a shallow relief or two-dimensional design on the surface of a cake or plaque. It can be straightforward or complicated, depending on the design chosen. Until proficient in this technique it is preferable to work on a plaque so that mistakes can be more easily corrected. This will have an added benefit as this technique is quite time consuming in that the plaque can be kept as a momento long after the cake has been eaten.

The principle is similar to a runout where the picture is created by completing the background first then working gradually forward.

For bas relief a combination of sugarpaste and modelling paste is used.

The sugarpaste is used principally for building up the main body of the design. The modelling paste (recipe page 12) is more pliable and is used to drape, cover or clothe the shapes or figures. As both pastes are quite soft, a modelling tool can be used to form depressions, creases and curves.

The main object is to mould and attach the clothing or covering in such a way that it appears to encircle the figure or shape, giving a three-dimensional effect.

For finishing details a number of techniques are used. Add the features and any patterning or shading on clothing with dusting colour and paint (food dye). Pipe in the hair. Paint the immediate foreground, add flowers and grasses using the modelling paste.

The three designs that have been carried out are given in order of difficulty: the Pierrot, the angel and finally the courting couple.

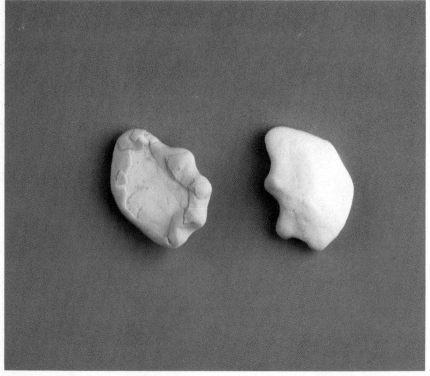

To give a more rounded effect in bas relief make the basic shape from white sugarpaste. When dry, cover the thinly rolled paste in the chosen colour for the design. The sleeves on the angel plaque on page 87 are made using this technique.

Basic shapes for the bas relief baby on the Christening cake.

Finished baby covered with a painted quilt.

Template

COURTING COUPLE CAKE

This cake would be ideal for an engagement cake, a small wedding cake or anniversary cake. The courting couple are made three-dimensional by using bas relief. The figures can be assembled directly on the cake top, or on a plaque which can then be removed and kept as a souvenir of the occasion. The pretty frills around the cake have been hand-painted to match the girl's dress.

Finished plaque

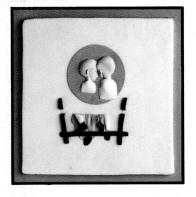

As the couple are worked straight onto the cake, it must be firm and dry. Cut out a large circle for the moon. Slightly depress girl's head where the boy's head is to be placed on top. Roll long sausages for fence posts. To complete background; paint grass, make flowers and paint with a very fine brush. Use the same flower pattern as on Garrett frill on girl's dress.

Flatten the backs or cut one sausage in half lengthwise to form two posts. Cut out lower edges of dress and tips of toes. Roll out and attach lower rail. The lower part of the legs are angled and should appear to protrude from the plaque. Model legs in sugarpaste, cutting away more and more paste as they recede into the picture. Drape with clothing. Pipe hair with stiff royal icing.

Make second rail. Build up upper bodies. Build up the boy's left shoulder slightly as this shoulder and arm will protrude more from the plaque as the arm is placed around the girl's shoulders.

Model skirt and trousers and position seated on rail. Make arms as for Pierrot and place in desired position. To add finishing touches; paint flowers on dress, stripes on trousers. Add bow to dress.

VALENTINE'S DAY PLAQUE

Finished plaque

Template

Flood the areas that will be in the background of the picture with royal icing; the balloon, the dress bodice and the shirt. Next flood the trouser legs and finally the main part of the trousers. Using paste or liquid food colour paint a heart on the balloon.

Using modelling paste, shape the heads. Cut the back of the head flat so that it sits on the plaque and does not protrude too much. Add ears and indent eye sockets using a ball tool. Add the arms, hands and feet. The hand holding the balloon is made in two stages; the palm of the hand and wrist are applied first, then the fingers are modelled from another piece of paste and added.

Roll out some paste thinly and, using a paper template, cut out and add the skirt and braces with buttons. Wrap some of the paste used for the dress around the top of the arm for the sleeve. Pipe in a belt between the skirt and bodice.

Make a tiny Garrett frill and attach to skirt hem. Place in eyes and nose. Add tails and attach arm with a little royal icing. To complete plaque, pipe the string on the balloon. Pipe some leaves and stems emerging from the boy mouse's hand. Add some small roses moulded around a stamen head. Make some whiskers from finely cut rice paper. Stick on with egg white.

TEDDY BEAR QUILT

Cut out the background shapes first: the bed and the bear's head and feet.

The inside of the pillow is modelled, allowed to dry, then painted with stripes before it is wrapped with the outer pillow-case.

Roughly shape some paste to represent the bulk of the teddy's body under the bedclothes. Drape the quilt over and tuck the edges well down to give a natural rounded look. Add wash set, honey pot and slippers.

Divide the quilt into squares and paint every other square. When dry paint the rest. Allow to dry. Paint on the surface pattern using a No000 brush. The wash jug and basin are painted in the same way.

Finished plaque

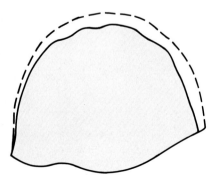

Template

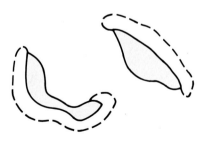

Quilt and Pillowcase. Heavy line (traced shapes from picture). Enlarge pattern to dotted edge to allow for overlap on pillow and tucking underneath and also to allow for added bulk.

Template

PIERROT

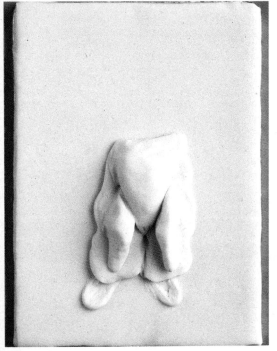

As this figure is a caricature the head and hands are not in correct proportion to the size of the body.

Roll out a piece of sugarpaste 1cm (⅜in) deep. Place the body pattern on paste and cut round. Moisten the underside and place on surface of plaque. Round off the cut edges with a finger. Add paste where the shape of the body needs to be more defined, e.g. the trunk and legs. Use a modelling tool to shape and round the body. Taper the legs to form ankles.

Apply a small sausage of sugarpaste to the toe area. Shape the foot with a modelling tool. Gradu-

ally depress the paste as it reaches the heel to give the impression that the foot is protruding from the plaque.

Cut out foot and shoe from white modelling paste. Place in position and smooth cut edge so that it adheres to the paste beneath. Indent a line where the shoe ends.

Thinly roll out another piece of white modelling paste for the Pierrot's costume. Make the pattern larger than the sugarpaste body to allow for the added paste. Moisten and drape over the sugarpaste. Use a modelling tool to drape the paste carefully around the body. Shape folds and

Finished
Pierrot plaque

creases. Round the cut edge so that the clothes appear to continue all round the figure.

Make the face by rolling out a piece of sugarpaste 5mm (¼in) thick. Roll two small balls of paste for the cheeks and make a triangle for the nose. Add to face. Make depressions for the eye sockets. (The eyes can be simply painted on later but indented eye sockets tend to make the face look more natural.)

Roll out another piece of flesh coloured modelling paste. Again, to allow for the extra paste added to the face, make the pattern slightly enlarged. Moisten and place over sugarpaste. Very care-fully, use a modelling tool to shape cheeks, nose and eye sockets.

Make arms of sugarpaste. Roll out modelling paste in white for sleeves. Cut out a large enough shape to wrap around the arm completely, add creases and folds. Moisten underside and attach alongside body and to plaque in the desired position.

Carefully model hands and place in cuff. Roll out paste for hat, cut out and attach.

Finish off figure by adding frills and pompoms. Paint hat and shoes black; paint in face. Model a rose and place in the hand.

Use the plaque on a child's birthday cake or other party cake.

Template

Finished plaque

Template for angel plaque

ANGEL

This pretty Christmas angel can be assembled directly on the cake top, or onto a plaque which can be removed and kept as a souvenir. The figure is made three-dimensional by the use of the bas relief technique. Final details are piped on with royal icing.

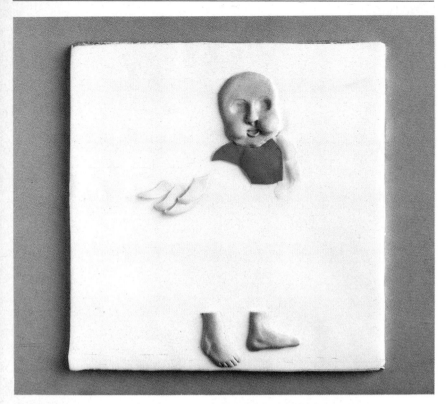

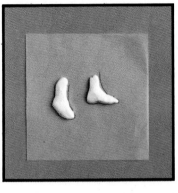

Trace the feet on silicone paper. Place a piece of sugarpaste on top and mould using the traced line as a guide. Cut out flesh coloured modelling paste slightly larger than the traced pattern to allow for added paste. Moisten, place over paste and shape with modelling tool. Use the back of a scalpel to make indented lines for toes.

Carefully transfer to plaque with a palette knife and with a modelling tool seal edge of plaque to give a smooth finish.

Cut feathers with scissors from thinly rolled blue paste. Cup edge on a piece of sponge. (This is the same method used for making flowers.) Start at base of wing with large feathers and work upwards making feathers gradually smaller. Overlap each row.

Make face as for Pierrot.

Slightly build up bodice with sugarpaste. Cut out bodice shape in modelling paste and apply as before.

Frill a long narrow piece of paste for petticoat. Apply to plaque. Cut out dress from pattern. Allow 2.5cm (1in) each side to allow for folding under and for making folds and creases.

Make each puff section of the sleeve separately. Work as for feet, keeping the shape within the confines of the traced line. Cut a large piece of blue paste and completely wrap around sugarpaste. Moisten and attach to plaque. Work from wrists upwards. Mark creases with modelling tool.

Carefully model two hands, paint face and add hair with firm royal icing. Finish off dress with royal icing.

MODELLING

Moulds are available for making modelled figures but more individual and lifelike results are gained by making them freehand and with an armature (wire support). This ensures that no two figures are alike. Each one takes on a personality of its own as choices of pose, features, dress and size are made.

Because the figures do vary in size and shape, the clothes patterns need to be adapted individually. Make the paste garments larger than needed so that the paste can be trimmed to shape as it is being draped around the form.

As the figure is dressed, it will increase in size, therefore the paste should be kept as thin as possible. Also the body shape should start off narrow to allow for the bulk of added clothes.

Accurate figure proportions are important. The head should measure one-sixth of the body height. In the case of a child, however, the head size is a little larger. Arms with outstretched fingers reach to mid-thigh.

Asking someone to pose will help to achieve a natural position.

A model made with a wire armature should not be used as a decoration on a cake for children or elderly people as they may attempt to eat it.

Painting the features

Eyes should focus on an object within the scene so they don't seem vacant or staring. Indent the socket and whiten. When dry paint the coloured iris. Dry, then place the pupil inside. A white dot can be added for a highlight. Carefully outline with a very fine brush, then add lashes and brows.

Blush cheeks with dusting powder. Paint lips a pale paprika colour; not bright pink or red.

Pipe hair with royal icing; or make by pushing soft paste through a garlic press or sieve. Alternatively, roll very thin sausages of paste into fine strands. This last method looks effective but is time consuming.

Each modelled part must be allowed to dry completely, otherwise it will crack and disintegrate when you try to dress it.

Views of the cottage in different stages
of assembling

GRANNY'S COTTAGE

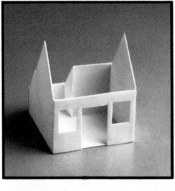

Cut out the pieces of the cottage following the templates on pages 94-95. Erect the house by joining walls to floor with royal icing which has had a pinch of gum tragacanth added for extra strength. Dust the interior walls and floor with a subtle toning colour.

Picture. Make a frame from brown paste, leave to dry, then paint a darker brown. Paint a small picture on a square of white paste the same size as the frame opening. Place frame over portrait and glue together. Attach to wall above the bed.

Carpet. Roll out a piece of paste thinly and cut out a square.

Bed. Roll white paste 5mm (¼in) thick and cut a rectangle for the mattress and a pillow. Indent the centre of the pillow for a head shape. Cut head and baseboard from brown paste. When dry paint a darker brown.

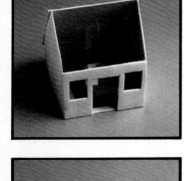

For the blanket use two pieces of paste, one yellow and a smaller white piece. Roll out both pieces thinly. Place the white piece on top of the yellow piece and roll together. When folded back the blanket will appear to have a sheet underneath. Drape the blanket over the bed and stick to the sides.

Now that the interior is completed the roof can be attached to the walls with royal icing.
Place the house on a green sugarpaste base.

When the furniture is in place carefully position the roof on top. Attach with royal icing.

Door. Make the door slightly larger than the door opening. Cut strips of paste and cut out notches to look like wooden planking; glue in place. Paint wood graining on each plank using a No0000 brush. Add a handle and hinges and place door in position with royal icing.

Exterior wooden framework. Roll out some brown paste quite thinly. Use a kitchen knife to cut into long strips. Stick horizontally to the house to form a pleasing pattern, making sure all corners are covered and the windows and door are framed. This will hide the seams.

Thatch. Colour a large amount of paste the colour of thatch, using dark cream with a little black. Roll out quite thickly. Use the same templates as for the roof but allow a little extra on each edge to overlap the roof beneath. Butt together at the top edge of the roof. Indent thatch marks using a tool made by cutting a slice of cork and pushing several pins through. As there is quite a large area of roof to cover, this tool will save time and give a better overall texture than using a single pointed tool.

Complete thatching by adding a long strip of paste to top of the roof, over-lapping each side. A cut pattern is made on each edge. Make thatch marks. The roof extension above both windows is made by rolling paste thickly at one edge and tapering it thinly at the other. Stick in position and make thatch marks, blending in well at the seams. The thatched area above the door is made in a thick shape so that it lodges down below window sections but fits neatly between them. Again make thatch marks and hide seams.

Chimney. Make bricks by rolling out some paste thinly and cutting it into strips with a kitchen knife. Cut the strips into small rectangles.
Mould two chimney pots; a barrel shape with a paintbrush handle inserted to hollow out. Leave to dry.
Make the chimney with a slightly rounded base. Stick in position on patterned thatch strip with royal icing. Glue on the bricks and attach chimney pots with royal icing. Dust each brick with colour to give a shaded effect.

Garden. Make a path in front of the door using gelatine crystals coloured with petal dust to give a sandy effect. Cover area with gum arabic or egg white, then sprinkle on crystals. Tip away excess.

The cobbled area is done by making small balls of paste that are flattened onto a glued surface.

Bushes, grasses and vine. Colour three or four pieces of paste in different shades of green.

The bushes are made by forcing a small piece of green paste through a garlic press.

Grass and the vine are made by pushing paste through a metal tea strainer with your thumb. Most of the grass grows around the edges of the house and between some of the cobbles to give a natural, slightly overgrown effect.

Make flowers using plunger cutters and push into the grass. The clinging vine breaks up the rigid framework on the side of the house.

Door   Back

Make templates for the walls and roof out of card. Roll out white paste, not too thinly, and cut around templates. Dry cutout pieces for a few days.

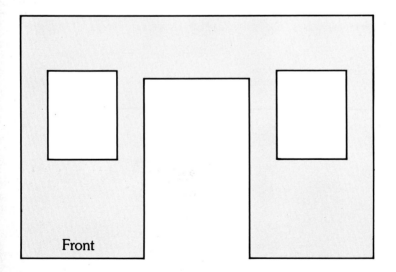

Front

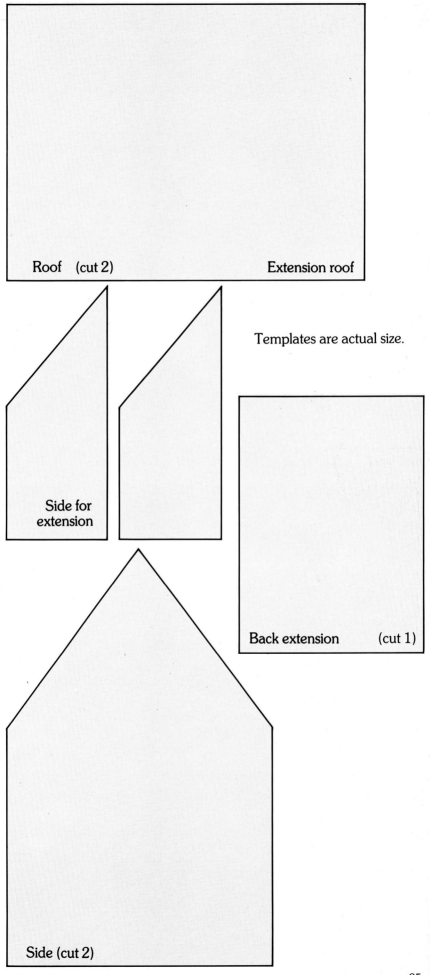

Roof   (cut 2)

Extension roof

Templates are actual size.

Side for
extension

Back extension   (cut 1)

Side (cut 2)

RED RIDING HOOD

Make the torso in a kneeling position. The arms and head are made separately.

Dress the body in finely rolled out blue paste, add an apron. Attach the arms with royal icing. Support them in position by using foam. Attach the head, paint in features, hair and shoes.

Roll out some red paste thinly; drape around figure. Make the hood separately and attach. Place some plunger flowers in her arms and attach one flower to a hand as if she is picking it.

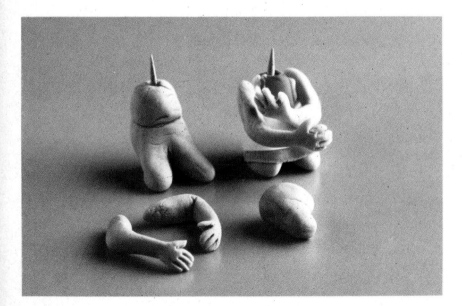

WOLF

Make a wire armature to support the figure. Begin with the chest area and build up the paste. Form the legs and push into the wire. Blend the paste on the thigh and the paste on the chest together with a modelling tool. Make the arms and attach in the same manner. Support arms with foam in the desired pose, dry. Attach the head and ears. Exaggerate the features to give a ferocious appearance. The texture of the fur is made by piping brown royal icing onto the figure in the direction the fur would grow. This also covers up joins and roughly blended areas.

APPLE CAKE

This charming novelty cake is
made in the shape of an enormous
apple. The mouse is life-sized.

MOUSE

Head is a small cone. Indent eyes, nostrils and a tiny mouth. For ears, press a ball of brown and a ball of flesh coloured paste together. Indent with ball tool. Pinch together base of ear and attach to head.

Texture the surface of the paste with a scalpel, or use royal icing piped onto the mouse and brushed to look like fur.

For back legs, make a ball, flatten and pull out to form top of leg. For front paws make a small cone; indent with little finger and curve to form arm. Make hands and feet with a small sausage of dark flesh colour. Flatten and cut four long, thin fingers and toes. Place on foam and indent with a ball tool to curve fingers. Attach to arms and legs with gum arabic glue. Blend with modelling tool.

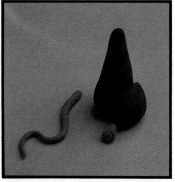

Make a long, thin sausage of dark flesh coloured paste for tail, tapering at one end. Using dark brown paste, make a thin pointed cone for body.

To make the fat mouse on the apple, make a large, fat cone. Position a cocktail stick to hold the head, and make the head as for the other mouse.

Make the paws, tail and ears as for the other mouse. Attach ears to head, but do not fix paws and tail until mouse is in place.

The apple leaves are finely rolled sugarpaste mixed with gum tragacanth. Frill the edges with a cocktail stick, and cut 'worm holes' with a piping tube. Attach to florist's wire.

The shape of the apple is made by moulding the marzipan around the cake. The indentations for the stem end and the eaten portion should be carved out of the cake. These cavities should be quite large as with each covering of marzipan and sugarpaste they will reduce in size.

Paint lines on the eaten portion of the apple with food colouring. Position the mouse, then attach his paws and tail.

TEDDY BEAR

Use sandy brown paste to make cone for body. Use a ball tool to indent sockets for arms and legs so they do not protrude too much from body.

Make a ball for head; indent eyes with ball tool. Cut out mouth with scalpel and open up with a pointed modelling tool. Attach nose, indent nostrils; place in tongue. For ears make a small ball, flatten, indent with ball tool. Pinch together bottom edge and attach to head, blending paste with modelling tool.

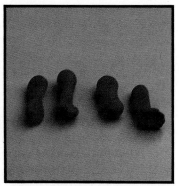

For arms and legs make a sausage, indent with little finger to shape. Cut toes and pad with scalpel. Attach with royal icing. Texture fur with scalpel. Pipe eyes. Paint eyes and nose when paste is dry.

SNOWMAN

Make a cone of white paste for the body and a ball for the head. Arms are two sausages, each indented at one end for mitts. Roll out a piece of coloured paste and cut a long, thin strip for scarf. Fringe each end and wrap around neck. Paint features. Indent a hole for the nose and insert a thin stick of orange paste for carrot. Indent a hole in mouth to hold pipe made of a tiny black sugarpaste sausage flattened at one end. Roll a large pea of black paste for hat. Shape into a cone.

With fingers pinch out bottom edge to form brim. Keep turning and pinching until hat takes shape. Indent top with a large ball tool. Pinch and furl brim. Make mitts of brightly coloured paste and place in arms. Make a long brown sausage for broom handle; leave to dry. For twigs, cut thin pieces of paste and stick together with royal icing or very sticky modelling paste. Hide join with a thin sausage of brown paste wrapped around the end of the twigs where they join the handle.

CAT

Make cone for body from sandy coloured paste. Cut a section up the front with a sharp knife, divide in two for legs. Pull legs downwards, indent and pinch to form feet. Cut toes. Make a ball

of paste for head. Indent eyes. Cut nose and mouth with scalpel. Open mouth with modelling tool. Add tongue. Cut a triangular piece of paste for ear. Pinch top corner, indent with ball tool, pinch the lower edge together and attach to head. Make a long sausage for tail; taper to a point at one end. Attach to body and drape over shoulder. When dry, paint stripes with paste food colour.

FATHER CHRISTMAS

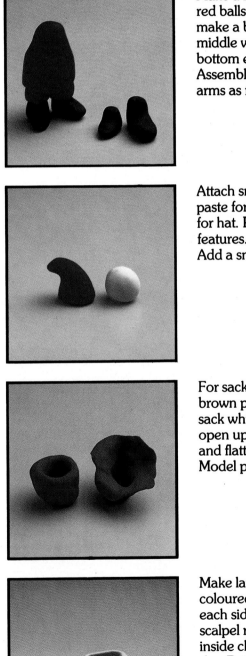

Make a red cone for body. Make two red balls and flatten for legs. For boots make a black sausage, indent in middle with little finger and flatten bottom edge of sole to give shape. Assemble body, legs and boots. Make arms as for Snowman.

Attach small ball of flesh coloured paste for head. Make cone of red paste for hat. Pinch top to give shape. Paint features. Pipe in beard and fur edging. Add a small ball of red paste for nose.

For sack, make a large fat sausage of brown paste. Indent with finger. Rotate sack while pinching with fingers to open up. Pinch two corners at base and flatten sack so that it will stand. Model presents and toys to fill.

Make large sausage in pale brick coloured paste for chimney. Flatten each side to form a square. With a scalpel remove a section of paste from inside chimney top. Leave chimney to dry. Paint in bricks with paste colour. Insert logs and boots or arm. Pipe snow with soft royal icing.

CHRISTMAS TREE

Make a tall cone. Using a sharp, fine bladed pair of scissors, cut paste into points. Start at the base and work upwards. The points become smaller towards the top of the tree. Make sure there are no gaps between them.

If the tree is made of green paste it can be decorated with coloured baubles of icing, parcels, and a star attached to the top point. Dredge with icing (confectioner's) sugar for a snowy effect. If the paste has not been coloured, dust with silver snowflake dusting powder.

SIMPLE CHOIR BOY

Shape a white cone for the surplice. Make a red sausage for the underskirt and flatten to the correct size. Attach underskirt to cone with egg white or gum arabic glue.

Make a long white sausage for arms. Measure against figure to obtain the correct length. Thin down the sausage where it crosses neck. Make indentations at the end of each arm. Make hands by rolling two small flesh coloured sausages. Flatten and curve with ball tool; place into indentations. Roll a flesh coloured ball for the head.

Make a frilled collar with a small carnation cutter. Frill edge with a cocktail stick. Place on body. Attach head. Make hair by cutting out a piece of yellow paste with a medium blossom cutter. Paint in eyes, nose and mouth. Roll out a thin white rectangle for the songsheet.

SIMPLE FAIRY OR ANGEL

Head is a small ball of flesh coloured paste. Hair and features are as for choir boy.

Make white cone for body. For arms, make two sausages from white paste, taper one end for shoulder. Indent sleeve end for hands. Model hands; completely curl one hand to hold the wand, which is made of florist's wire with a tiny cutout sugarpaste star stuck on the end.

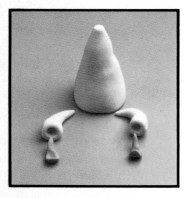

Cut wings from white paste using a large rose petal cutter. Attach to back of cone with royal icing. Decorate edges of dress with piped dots of royal icing.

ELABORATE CHOIR BOY

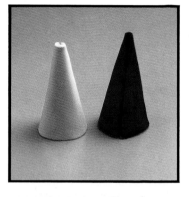

Roll out red paste 2mm (⅛in) thick. Make a cone, leave to dry.

Roll out white paste thinly for surplice. Cut lower edge with No2 and 3 writing tubes. Attach to cone.

To make arms, taper one end of a flesh coloured sausage and flatten to form a spade shape. Cut out thumb and fingers. Roll with index finger and thumb to form wrist, elbow and upper arm. Leave to dry. Wrap red paste around arm to form sleeve. Cut out surplice sleeve from white paste. Make patterned edge as for bottom of surplice. Drape sleeve around arm and attach to body with royal icing.

Make ball for head. Pinch a nose. Indent eyes slightly. Make mouth by inserting cocktail stick into the paste. When dry, paint features. Dust cheeks a rosy colour. Pipe some hair with royal icing. Make frilled collar by cutting out two shapes with a small carnation cutter. Frill edges with cocktail stick; place on cone.

ELABORATE FAIRY OR ANGEL

The method is similar to that for the elaborate choir boy. Make cone base of white paste. The dress is made from four pattern shapes cut from thin white paste. Frill edges by indenting with a cocktail stick. Attach in order as numbered. Shape arms. Cut out sleeves and frill. Drape over arms; attach to shoulders with royal icing. Frill collar and attach. Make head as for choir boy. Wings are cut out of rice paper and attached with royal icing. Place wand in hand.

Main cone

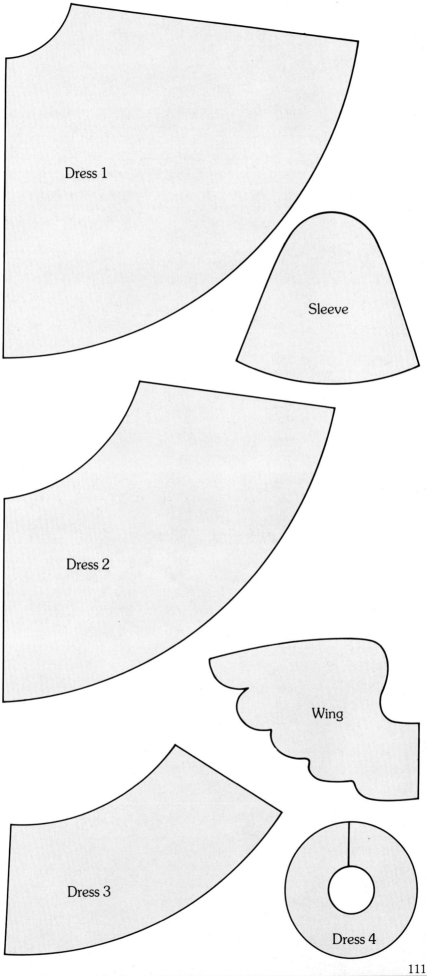

HANSEL AND GRETEL AND THE WITCH

These fantastic sugarpaste
models, shown here at actual
size, could be placed on a large
cake or used as a centrepiece for
a children's party.

HANSEL AND GRETEL

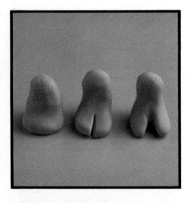

Model bodies using flesh coloured paste. Gretel's seated body does not need a support. Make a cone, indent with finger to form waist. Cut lower half of cone to form knees. Smooth and round off.

Make heads for both figures by cutting a small doll in half and making a plaster mould. This ensures that the details on the faces will be identical for brother and sister. Attach Gretel's head to body.

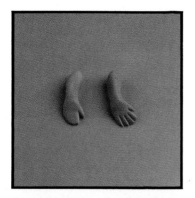

Model the hands and arms. Taper one end of a sausage and flatten to form a spade shape. Cut out a small 'V' for the thumb, then cut fingers. Separate each finger and smooth tips to round. Place on a piece of foam and curve fingers by drawing a ball tool over them towards the palm. Indent palm with ball tool. Form wrist, elbow and upper arm by rolling paste with finger. Place in a natural pose and dry.

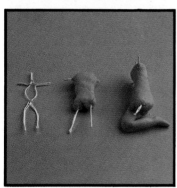

Hansel's kneeling figure will need a wire support. Mould paste around 28-gauge wire.

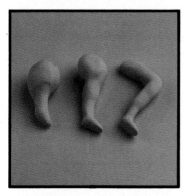

Model legs and push onto wire. Blend paste on top of leg to thigh. Trim away excess or add more paste until the correct shape is achieved. Support the body until dry.

The arms and lower legs will be visible so they should be smooth and well formed. The main torso will be hidden by clothes.

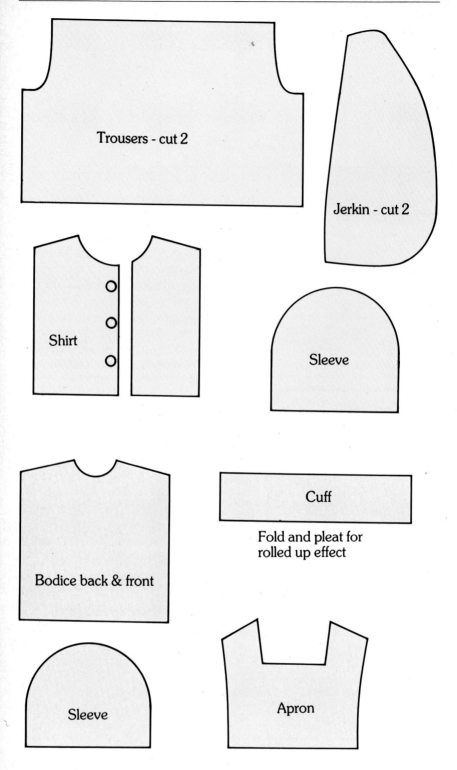

Trousers - cut 2

Jerkin - cut 2

Shirt

Sleeve

Bodice back & front

Cuff

Fold and pleat for
rolled up effect

Sleeve

Apron

Cut out a front and back bodice from
thin paste and drape on Gretel. Frill
the bottom of a rectangular piece of
paste for skirt. Place on figure. Drape a
small piece of paste around upper arm
for sleeve. Attach arms to body. Paint
in features. Dress and finish Hansel
figure as for Gretel. Make lollipops of
brightly coloured paste as for Witch.

WITCH

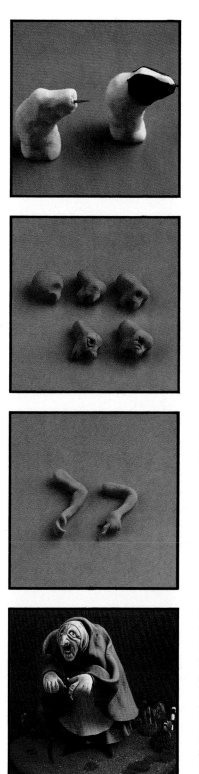

Shape the body so that it is hunched over as shown.

Make a ball of paste for head. Make face with exaggerated features. Pinch out nose, indent eyes and pinch close together. Make creases and wrinkles with a modelling tool. Attach to body with royal icing.

Model arms and hands. Elongate fingers and exaggerate bony shoulders and elbows. Allow to dry. Attach to body with royal icing.

Cut a skirt from a rectangular piece of paste. Drape round body and trim away excess. Make folds and creases with a modelling tool. Model shoes and place on base. Paint in features. Roll lollipops of brightly coloured paste. Make a hole and allow to dry. Roll sticks from tiny sausages of paste. Glue in lollipop hole. Complete plaque with grass and sandy areas as for House.

PUSS IN BOOTS

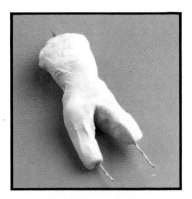

As this is a large piece of modelling it will need a heavy plaque base. Make a wire armature for the body using 24-gauge wire. Mould paste around the wire. Exaggerate chest, keep waist narrow and slightly build up sides of thighs. Leave to dry.

Model arms, paws and tail. Place in desired position, paint details of fur and leave to dry. Dress figure.

Mould face. Pinch nose, indent eyes and open up mouth. Model one ear and attach to head.

Leave to dry, then attach head to body with royal icing. Paint features.

For boots, make a fat sausage of brown paste, indent centre with finger and bend in half. Model one end to form foot by working on a flat surface. Pinch in toe and round heel. Place a modelling tool inside top of boot and start to open. Keep pinching and turning the boot until it is the desired height. If the top has frilled too much, make a pleat on the inside. To make cuff, cut a thin strip of paste and glue inside top of boot. Round off top edge. Make creases with a modelling tool to give a worn look. Attach arms to body. Paint details on clothing, stripes on trousers, etc. For sack, make a large ball of earthy or sandy brown paste. Start pinching top edge, open up slightly with a modelling tool. Make creases and bulges. Arrange to sag against Puss's boot.

Make a ball of paste for hat. Roll into a thick sausage, pinch out top. Keep turning and pinching until the brim is the desired size and thickness. Open up crown with a ball tool. Indent top with finger and pinch together. Place on Puss's head and tilt front brim at a rakish angle. Add buttons, scarf, belt and buckle, hat band, tongue, etc. Sprinkle coloured gelatine crystals on plaque for path and muddy area. Add grass and moss of green paste.

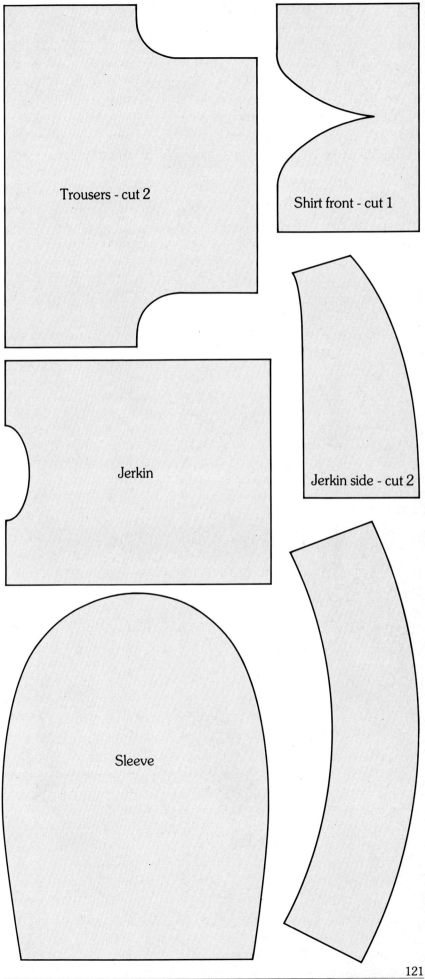

Trousers - cut 2

Shirt front - cut 1

Jerkin

Jerkin side - cut 2

Sleeve

MOULDED SUGARPASTE FLOWERS

Choose simple unfussy flowers to mould from sugarpaste as it does not dry to the same firmness as flower paste which is more commonly used. Sugarpaste flowers can't be wired, nor can they be thinned down to the same delicacy.

Moulded flowers made and assembled using patty tins or polystyrene apple trays are ideal as this way they are protected and supported.

When dry and ready for use the flowers are arranged directly on the cake with leaves placed between and around them.

Other flowers that can be made using this method are buttercup, poinsettia, pansy and anemone.

Christmas rose
Make petals as for briar rose but use a smaller pea of paste. If paste is sticky when removed from the polythene, dust with a little cornflour (cornstarch) before cupping with a ball tool. Place petals on calyx one at a time with last petal overlapping the fourth petal and tucked under first petal. Pipe a dot of royal icing and add stamens.

Briar or dog rose
When pressing between polythene, try to make a heart shaped petal. Press one side of the top first, then the other side. Cup with ball tool and slightly furl back the top edges of the petal using a paintbrush handle or cocktail stick, depending on the size of the petal. Assemble petals on calyx. When dry dust centre greenish yellow and pipe a dot of royal icing. Colour stamens.

Poppy
Colour some sugarpaste red. Add a little cornflower blue to turn an orangey red into a rich ruby colour. Poppy petals are much larger than rose petals and will need to harden off a bit in an egg container before assembly. Make a stigma with a slightly flattened ball of green paste. Pipe a wheel on top. Attach with a dot of royal icing and place black stamens around base.

INSTRUCTIONS FOR CAKES

Heart cake. Bake cake in a heart shaped tin and cover with coloured sugarpaste. Emboss with crimper work as detailed on page 19. Make orchids and attach as shown.

Wedding bell cake. Bake cake in a bell shaped tin and cover with white sugarpaste. Insert ribbon according to the instructions on page 21. Add frills, flowers and piping as shown.

Garrett frill christening cake.
Add frill to outer edge. Model
baby's head and shape body.
Roll out a large piece of paste and
cut into a rectangle for quilt and
blanket. Paint on flowers. Add
frilled edge and ribbon.

To apply Garrett frill to cake:
scribe a mark on the cake where
frill is to be placed. Work lower
frill on each corner of cake. Apply
second row on each corner. Frill
the final continuous row.

Cake with drape. Instructions
for applying the drape are found
on page 37. Finish cake and
board as shown.

Parcel cake. Cut out coloured shapes in sugarpaste. Roll out more sugarpaste to cover the cake. Place the cutouts on the sugarpaste before it starts to skin. Place a piece of waxed or grease-proof paper over the cutouts, then roll over the area *once* quite firmly. Remove the paper and cover the cake in the usual way.

Fox cub cake. Coat cake and board with marbled beige and brown coloured sugarpaste. Add ribbon banding as shown. Make fox cub plaque on page 54. Attach to cake with royal icing.

Cat cake. Mark the position of the cat. Do not mark out the other details as these are painted freehand. The background tones are quite muted and the colours become stronger towards the foreground. The flowers and leaves are moulded and positioned last to complete the three-dimensional effect.

Clock cake. Instructions for making the collars and assembling the Clock cake are on page 70.

126

Courting couple cake.
Instructions for this cake are
found on page 78.

Apple mouse cake. Use a
generous layer of marzipan when
covering an awkward shape to
eliminate all rough edges and
bumps where the cake has been
carved. Make any cavities larger
than needed as each covering of
sugarpaste will reduce its size.
The marzipan can be built up or
carved away at this stage to
perfect the shape.

Fix the marzipanned cake to a
board and cover completely with
sugarpaste. Support paste with
the hands as it is gently eased into
the cavities. Cut away excess at
base and smooth well with hands.
Use a large soft brush to colour
with red paste colour diluted with
a little water and tinted with a bit
of brown and green colour for a
redish-rust shade. Use large
downward strokes; don't have
the brush too wet. Copy a real
apple for shading and detail.

Apply thinly rolled out cream
coloured paste to the bite mark;
indent with modelling tool to
form marks. Paint marks a rust

colour. Pinch out paste on edge
to look like torn apple skin. Make
stalk and leaves and add to top of
apple. Make mouse body; then
model head with pointed face.
Indent eyes with small ball tool.
Attach to body with royal icing.
Make arms and let dry. Add
thighs to side of body. Model feet
and place under body. Attach
arms to sides with royal icing.
Make a small piece of apple and
attach to hands with royal icing.